WRITE YOUR S

What comes first - the pictures or the story? If you guessed the story, you're right! The story comes first because the actions that you will draw will come from the ideas in your story.

What do you want to write about? You can make up anything you want. You may choose to use examples from your own life to help you with your story. Write about your adventures or maybe a dream. This is your story, be as creative as you want. Get started now by writing below.

Comic Book Name:_____

Tips

The name should reflect the story. For example, a book about robots could be called Warbots.

Make sure you let the reader know what your character is like, where they come from & what they do.

To make your story exciting and interesting, you should create a problem for your main characters to overcome.

For example, your character realizes that Earth is under attack by Martians & they have to save the world!

Add conversations you'll have with friends & enemies.

This part takes up most of the pages of your comic book so you should have <u>lots</u> to write about.

Remember to create a dramatic ending for your story. This will make your story more memorable and enjoyable for your readers.

Introduction

Main Action

Conclusion

CREATE YOUR CHARACTER

Now that you've finished writing your story, who are the main characters and what can they do?

Fill out the sheet below to help you to keep track of the characters in your adventure. You should do this for every person in your story. Use a blank piece of paper for the other characters. Remember, to be a true super-hero you need to have a really cool name!

1) Character Name:_____

2) Character Age:_____

3) Character Features:_____

4) Be sure to think about the other parts of your character(s). What are their super powers, hobbies and who are their friends?

DRAWING YOUR FACE

To draw your face, begin with an oval and add guidelines - one down the middle of the face and the other across the face to show you where to place the eyes and ears.

DETAILING YOUR CHARACTER'S FACE

Facial detail is very important and will change according to how your character is feeling. Your character may be happy, sad or angry, and this will change the way the mouth and eyes will look.

FACIAL SIDE VIEW

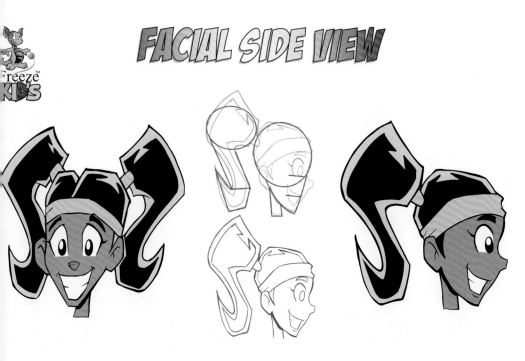

FACIAL PROFILES

Draw the side view of a character as well as the front view for a greater understanding of the characters.

HANDS

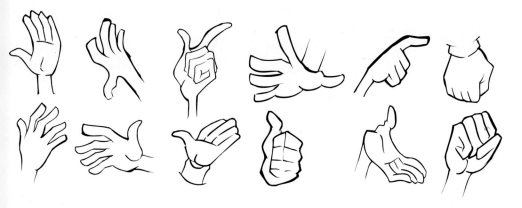

DRAWING HANDS

Here are some examples of different hand poses.
Drawing hands can be very difficult. You can use your own hand as a reference model.
For more examples check out www.freeze-kids.com.

FACIAL EXPRESSIONS

TRY TO DRAW YOUR CHARACTERS WITH AS MANY
EXPRESSIONS AS YOU CAN. THESE CAN BE USED LATER,
WHEN ILLUSTRATING YOUR COMIC BOOK.

Here are some examples of facial expressions
that can be used for girl or boy characters.

HAPPY

ANGRY

EMBARRASSED

LAUGHTER

NERVOUS

WORRIED

SCARED

GLAD

MAD

SCREAMING

STEP 1: Layout Of Your Character

First you will need to draw the head. Draw an oval near the top of the page and then continue down the page until you have completed all of the ovals like the example.

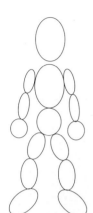

STEP 2: Outline Of Your Character

Now you have to form the shape of the body by adding curves. You should also include basic details. Begin by putting in smaller ovals for the shoulders, elbows, wrists, knees and ankles. Don't forget the fingers!

STEP 3: Detailing Your Character

In this step you have to add fine details to your character. For example, adding in the hair, drawing a sweater and everything else your character needs.

STEP 4: Inking Your Character

Inking is when you trace over the pencil lines with a pen to give your character a finished look. Only ink over the lines that you need to use! Once you have finished inking your character, erase any left over pencil lines.

REMEMBER:
Draw lightly so that you can erase the lines later!

STEP 5: Coloring Your Character

Decide what colors you want to use for your characters. Now color your character in. Make sure you use the same colors for your character every time you draw them. Think about what happens in your story and what colors you will need later for the back-grounds. If your story takes place under-water, you're going to need a lot of blue and light green.

CHARACTER DESIGN

Here are a couple of different kinds of characters you can design.

Things to consider:
Hairstyles and type of clothing. Are your characters human, animal, or something totally different?

REMEMBER:
Choose colors that will compliment all the aspects of the characters personality.

Things to consider:
Does your character get mad a lot? Are they sea creatures, or do they fly?

HEROES

Heroes should be strong and ready to save the world! They should also have a weakness.   Your story will be more interesting if the reader is not sure of the outcome.

SIDEKICKS

Every super hero has an even better sidekick. Someone who helps solve crimes and is always there to save your hero when they are in a jam! Your sidekick can be human or a funny little creature.

SIGNATURE Jamie watson

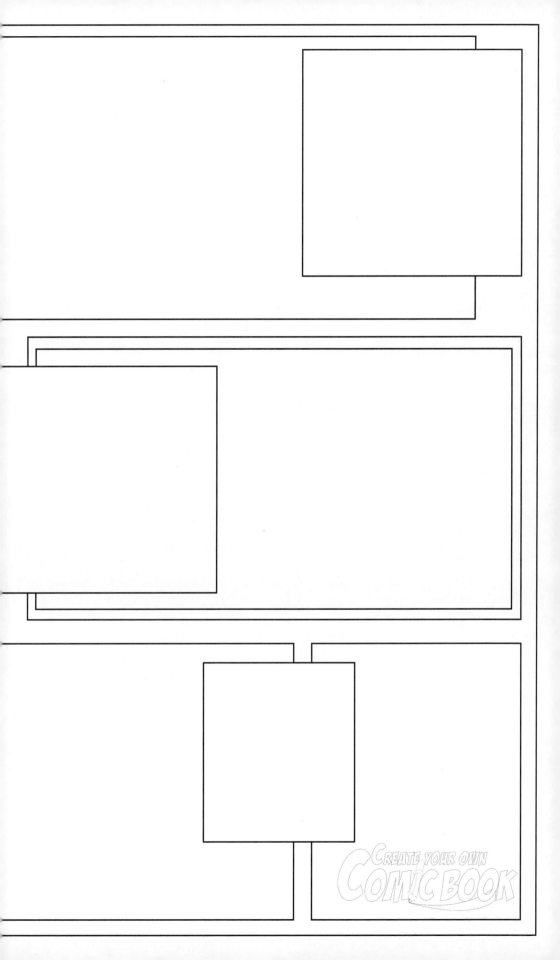

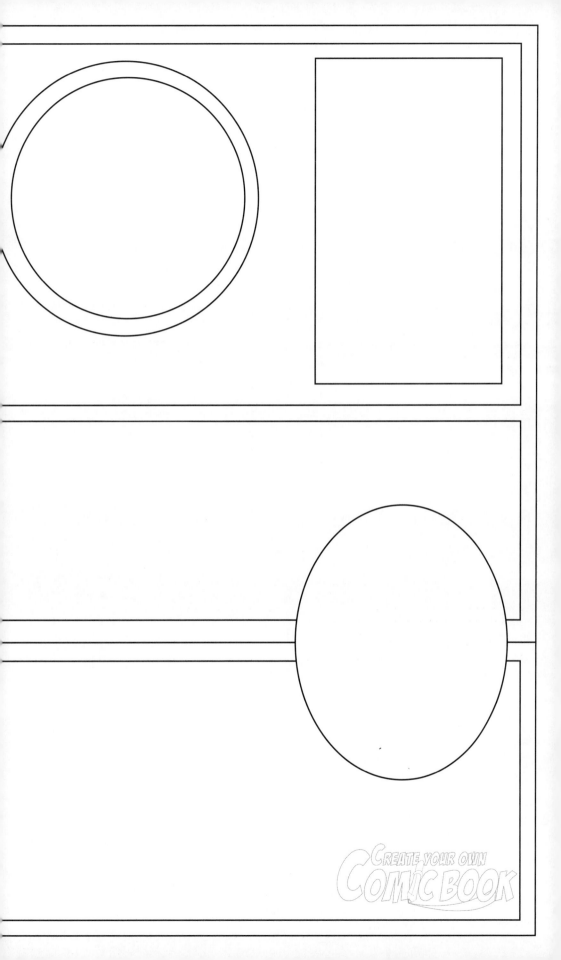

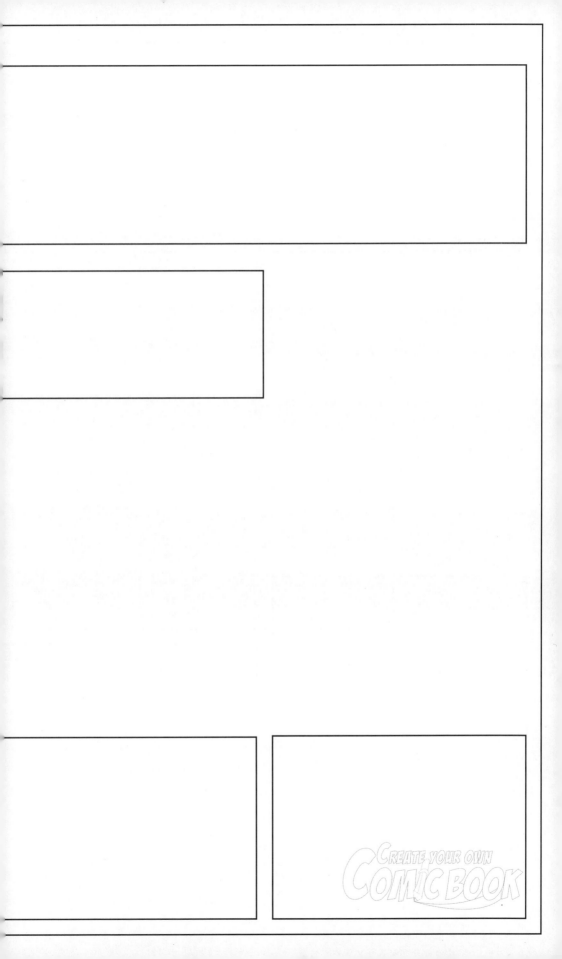

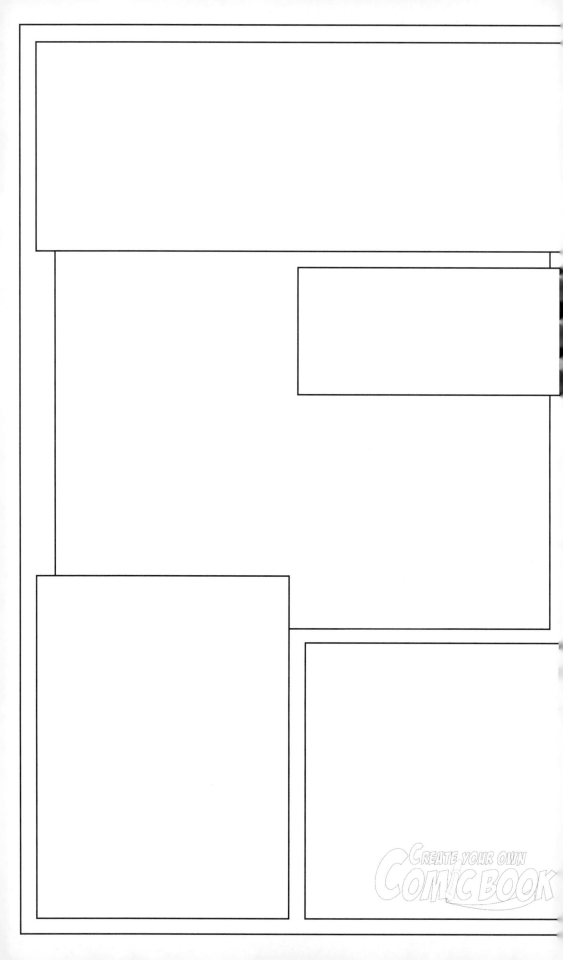

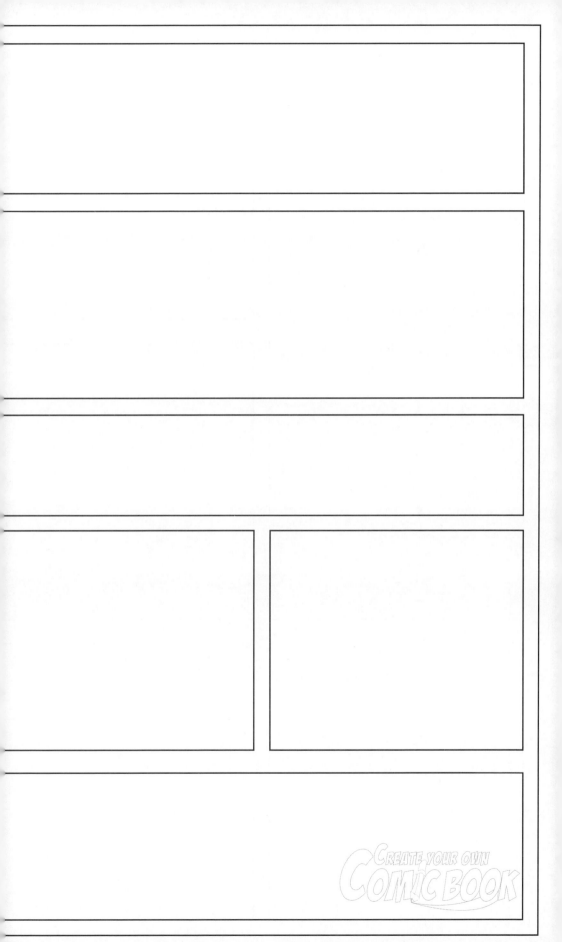

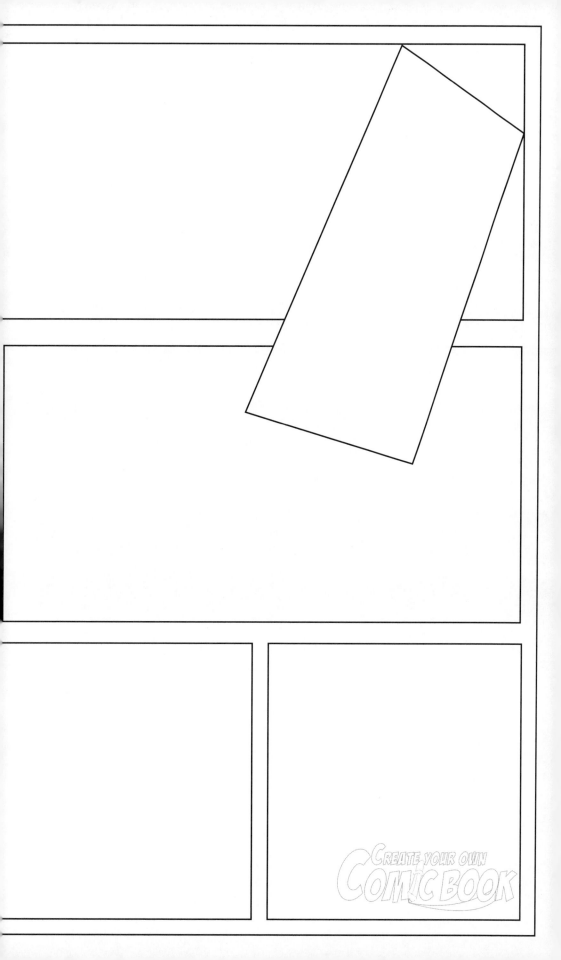

VILLAINS

VILLAINS

Your villains should appear invincible! Their weakness should only be revealed at the end of your story. Most villains appear as though they have no doubts that they will be victorious!

REMEMBER:
The hero and villain will have many encounters in your story. Make sure they are explosive and exciting!

THE MOST IMPORTANT DETAIL ABOUT YOUR HEROES AND VILLAINS IS HOW THEY GOT THEIR POWERS. DID THEY GET STRUCK BY LIGHTNING? WAS IT A FREAKY DNA MIX UP IN THE SCHOOL SCIENCE LAB? THESE DETAILS ARE WHAT WILL SHAPE YOUR CHARACTER'S PERSONALITY AND POWERS.

9

WORD BUBBLES

WORD BUBBLES ARE USED TO SHOW YOUR CHARACTERS SPEAKING AND THINKING. THERE ARE DIFFERENT KINDS OF WORD BUBBLES TO USE.

STANDARD BUBBLES:
These are used when the character is talking. Note: The pointy part of the bubble should point at the character's mouth.

OVERLAPPING BUBBLES:
These are for conversations between two or more characters. The character who talks first should have their word bubble on top.

ACTION BUBBLES:
These are used to show the emotion of the character like anger, surprise and fear.
The letters are usually larger and darker.

THOUGHT BUBBLES:
These are used when a character thinks something but doesn't say it out loud.
They can also be used for animals since they cannot speak.

ACTION WORDS

You can combine your drawings with sound effects by adding action words. They are similar to *Action Bubbles*, but they are sounds not words.

THUMP   SPLASH   BANG   CREAK

SQUEAK   CRASH   ZOOM

POW   KABOOM   SHHH

1. Design a storyboard.

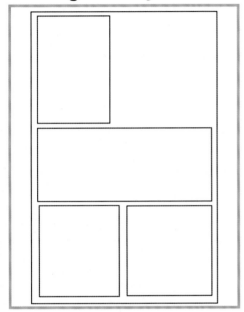

2. Draw two people talking.

3. Put in word bubbles.

4. Ink and color.

MOST STORYBOARDS HAVE 4-6 PANELS. THIS MAKES YOUR PAGE EASY TO READ! YOU CAN MAKE A BASIC STORYBOARD BY DIVIDING THE PAGE INTO EQUAL PANELS.

What are storyboards?

Storyboards are the pages in the comic where all the action happens. Each storyboard has little windows that are called panels. You use the panels to draw the different parts of the story.

How do storyboards tell the story?

Panels and drawings have to follow the order of the story. Make sure you plan each page so that your storyboard shows what's happening. You have to decide what pictures will go first, second, third and so on. Each page should have a maximum of six panels. The story has to go from left to right and top to bottom. Be sure to think about the backgrounds (for example, buildings or a park) and the views (the way you are looking at the scene - straight-on or from above).

Basic Storyboard

HOW TO MAKE STORYBOARDS

Advance Storyboarding

To give more style, you can make the panels uneven. Try changing the length and width of each panel to make it more eye-catching.

Professional Storyboard

Instead of drawing flat lines to divide each panel, try making diagonal ones.

By overlapping the panels and tilting them, your comic will have a dynamic look.

Another way to make your comic look cool is to have borderless panels.

COVER PAGES CAN BE THE COOLEST PART OF THE COMIC BOOK! THEY ARE IMPORTANT BECAUSE THEY GET THE READER INTERESTED. THEY SHOULD SHOW WHAT'S SPECIAL ABOUT YOUR STORY.

Logo

You need a logo! A logo is the symbol that represents your comic. For example, this book is about drawing your own comic book, so our logo looks like this:

All you need to do is use the name of your comic and attach shapes to it that reflect the story.

For example, we used a pencil in the Create Your Own Comic Book logo.

Cover Picture

This is just like drawing a panel.

1) Lightly pencil out a sketch of the main character(s) in the book.

2) Start to ink over the pencil drawings.

3) Add colors to the cover. Keep in mind that the colors should match the style of your book (action drawings should have bright colors).

4) Don't forget your signature!
It goes in the bottom right-hand corner.

Leave space for your logo and the issue number.

Company Name

Last but not least you need to create a company name for yourself.

You are about to create a whole series of comics so they should all have your name. Choose your name based on yourself or something to do with your comic book adventure.

CONGRATULATIONS ON COMPLETING YOUR FIRST COMIC BOOK! YOU ARE NOW AN OFFICIAL FREEZE KIDS DESIGNER. BE SURE TO SHARE YOUR ADVENTURES WITH OTHERS AND KEEP CREATING!

USE THESE OUTLINE SAMPLES TO PRACTICE. YOU CAN TRACE THEM AND CREATE YOUR OWN CHARACTERS.

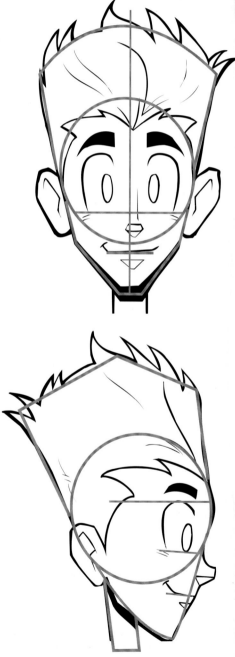